For You – From My Heart

PRESS

For You – From My Heart
by B. Allen

Printed in the United States of America

ISBN-13: 978-1-60034-207-3
ISBN-10: 1-60034-207-8

www.xulonpress.com

Table of Contents

Introduction

*T*his small book is addressed to Muslims and Christians in an effort to increase understanding between people of the Muslim and Christian faiths. In 2001, I was given the opportunity to live and work in Bangladesh. In that Muslim country, religion and what a person believes are often some of the first topics of discussion when meeting people. Several years earlier I had been treated as a special guest in the home of Muslims in Indonesia and in Iran. In the same way, Bangladeshi Muslims proved to be just as friendly and hospitable. Having recently arrived in Bangladesh, I wanted to get a better understanding of the Muslim faith that impacts all facets of life in any Muslim country. I therefore read the entire Qur'an over the Korbani Eid holiday in 2002. As I read the Qur'an, I was amazed at how much Muslims and Christians have in common according to their scriptures. In fact, the Qur'an is about the same size as the Christian New Testament. I would encourage Christians to consider reading it as I did. A copy can be obtained from IB Publisher, Inc. at info@ibpublisher.com.

As the author of this small book, it seems appropriate that the reader should know something of my background. I was born and raised in the United States of America in close connection with a church and a system of beliefs that most of the world would label as "Christian." I did not understand the Christian faith and I was not a believer. I had been taught that my salvation from sin depended on the success of my own efforts in following religious rules and regulations. I joined the military and during that time met people that called themselves Christians. They told me that I could never be "good" enough to earn my way to heaven, that Jesus died to pay the debt for my sins, and that only by turning my life over to Jesus would I be able to see heaven. I had no interest in what they were saying and I rejected what they were telling me.

After I was released from the military the question of whether God existed—and if so, what difference it made in my life—plagued me. This was due to a visit I had late one night as I was driving across the country and had pulled off the road to sleep. Hours later three young men came to my car and tried to tell me about Jesus. I told them that I was not interested in what they had to say. One of the three young men came back a little later and asked me to consider that if there was only one chance in a million that their words were true, then was it not worth checking out?

Months later, having moved to Australia, I began to look for spiritual truth. I challenged God to prove that He is real. He did that beyond any doubt in 1978 when my search kept me returning to hear a man speak to people about Jesus. He would always close the meeting by asking if anyone wanted to step forward and accept Jesus into their heart. As the days passed, I understood this man to be speaking the truth and I decided to give my life to Jesus. At the next meeting I accepted Jesus and became a believer. About one week later, while in prayer, I asked Jesus to take away the desire for alcohol that still tempted me from my old life. Before I had finished uttering the prayer in my heart, the Lord removed the desire for alcohol and I have been free from that desire ever since that moment.

This small book highlights the large amount of scriptural common ground between Muslims and Christians as well as the single main point on which they differ. Therefore, the substance of this book is primarily quotations from the Qur'an and from the Bible in a topical format. Scriptural citations are provided so that the reader is able to verify quotations in addition to being able to see the context from which the quotation came.

The English quotations of the Qur'an are taken from the English translation by Abdullah Yusuf Ali, Goodword Books, 2001 printing. (permission to quote requested from Goodword Books Pvt. Ltd. with the response noting it is in the Public Domain). The English quotations of the Bible are taken from the New International Version. (Scripture taken from the HOLY BIBLE, NEW INTERNATIONAL VERSION®. Copyright© 1973, 1978, 1984 by International Bible Society. Used by permission of Zondervan Publishing House. All rights reserved.)

In the Christian scripture, known as the "Bible," what is called the Old Testament (including the Taurat-Torah and Zabur-Psalms) contains scripture written before Jesus Christ and the New Testament (referred to as the "Injil" by Muslims) contains scripture given after Jesus Christ. Therefore, the Old Testament and the New Testament together make up the complete Christian Bible.

The names "God" and "Allah" are used interchangeably herein. The historical support for the use of "Allah" as the name for the only one true Supreme Being predates the use of "God" which is derived from the German language. Western scholars are fairly unanimous that the source of the word 'Allah' probably is through Aramaic from the Syriac 'alaha' (the God). In either case, the Arabs used the word 'Allah' for the Supreme Being before the time of Muhammad. Moreover, inscriptions with Allah have been discovered in Northern and Southern Arabia from as early as the fifth century BC. Arabic Christians have used the name 'Allah' from pre-Islamic times and 'Allah' has been used continuously in Arabic translations of the Bible from the earliest known versions in the eighth century to this day. The foregoing is adapted from "Allah in Translations of the Bible" (Thomas, K.J.,UBS Translation Consultants, New York 2001).

The reader is encouraged to verify the verses that follow in the holy books for themselves and to read the verses before and after the quotation to obtain the full context of the meaning. Verses from the Qur'an are in italics and verses from the Bible are in bold. Abbreviated quotations are used here to convey the meaning in a precise and easy-to-read manner. Consequently, this small book can be read in as little as fifteen minutes.

Similarly, Muslims should consider reading the Bible, or at least the New Testament portion which tells about the life of Jesus. A copy can be obtained from most Christians, churches or a Christian book store.

Since this short work is an effort to highlight where verses from the Muslim and Christian holy books agree, and in one case disagree, the first few points will underscore the authenticity and validity of the Christian verses from a Muslim and Christian perspective.

1.

No one is able to change Allah's word

The Qur'an says:

The Cattle 6:34 …there is none that can alter the words (and decrees) of Allah.

The Cattle 6:115 …None can change his words: For he is the one who hears and knows all.

Jonah 10:64 …No change can there be in the words of Allah. This is the supreme felicity.

The Cave 18:27 And recite (and teach) what has been revealed to you of the Book of your Lord: none can change his words ….

The Bible says:

Deuteronomy 4:2 Do not add to what I command you and do not subtract from it, but keep the commands of the Lord your God that I give you.

Proverbs 30:5,6 Every word of God is flawless; he is a shield to those who take refuge in him. Do not add to his words, or he will rebuke you and prove you a liar.

Revelation 22:18,19 I warn everyone who hears the words of the prophecy of this book: if anyone adds anything to them, God will add to him the plagues described in this book. And if anyone takes words away from this book of prophecy, God will take away from him his share in the tree of life and in the holy city, which are described in this book.

2.

Allah's word cannot be corrupted

The Qur'an says:

The Table Spread 5:46-50 And in their footsteps we sent Jesus the son of Mary, confirming the Law that had come before him: we sent him the Gospel: therein was guidance and light, and confirmation of the Law that had come before him....

Jonah 10:94 If you are in doubt as to what we have revealed unto you, then ask those who have been reading the Book from before you....

The Bible says:

Isaiah 40:8 The grass withers and the flowers fall, but the word of our God stands forever.

Matthew 24:35 (Jesus said) Heaven and earth will pass away, but my words will never pass away.

3.

Allah is One — all powerful and all knowing

The Qur'an says:

The Cattle 6:17 If Allah touch you with affliction, none can remove it but He: If He touch you with happiness, He has power over all things.

The Repentance 9:51 Say: "Nothing will happen to us except what Allah has decreed for us: He is our protector."

The Bible says:

Deuteronomy 6:4 Hear, O Israel: The Lord our God, the Lord is one.

Psalms 103:19 The Lord has established his throne in heaven, and his kingdom rules over all.

Psalms 135:6,7 The Lord does whatever pleases him, in the heavens and on the earth, in the seas and all their depths. He makes clouds rise from the ends of the earth; he sends lightning with the rain and brings out the wind from his storehouses.

Mark 12:29 "The most important one (commandment)," answered Jesus, " is this: Hear, O Israel, the Lord our God, the Lord is one...."

In consideration of the foregoing verses, Muslims and Christians can agree that Allah's word is unchangeable, Allah's word is uncorrupted and that Allah is sovereign. Some claim the Christian and Jewish scriptures have been changed. Muslims, Christians and Jews would not have allowed this to occur. In Muhammad's time, the Bible had been completely or partially translated into many languages and only portions of the Christian scriptures were available in Arabic. Muhammad encouraged Muslims to read the Christian and Jewish scriptures. Any change of scripture after the time of Muhammad would have had to include a coordinated conspiracy between people of many different languages and cultures. The effort would have required Jewish and Christian believers to come together to agree on how to change scripture. Tens of thousands of copies of scripture were scattered all over the known world at the time of Muhammad. The destruction of all copies would have been required. In fact, there has never been, nor will there ever be a successful change or corruption of scripture.

Partial or complete copies of Christian scriptural manuscripts are available today in the following number: more than 5,000 Greek manuscripts, 10,000 Latin manuscripts and thousands of manuscripts in other languages. The foregoing is adapted from "Handbook to Exegesis of the New Testament" (Porter, S.E., Brill Academic Publishers, Leiden 1997). These manuscripts date from about AD 120, only 20 years following the last *original* writing — and the earliest complete manuscript dates from AD 350. It should be noted that in recent decades, a number of different new English translations have become available where the words may differ but the content remains the same.

The exact locations of ancient New Testament (Injil) manuscripts are known. One of the most noteworthy, the Codex Vaticanus (AD 325) has been in the Vatican library since the late 1400s. The Codex Sinaiticus (AD 350) was given by monks in Sinai to the Czar of Russia in the 1860s. It was purchased by the British Museum in 1933. The Codex Alexandrinus was written around the fifth century and is kept at the British Museum. It contains the entire Greek Bible except for forty lost leaves. The foregoing is adapted from "An Introduction to the Old Testament in Greek. Additional Notes" (Swete, H.B., Hendrickson Publishers, Peabody 1989). Many other manuscript fragments exist which predate these. All of these ancient copies, manuscripts and fragments agree completely with current modern editions. Allah's Word has not been changed – it cannot be changed.

As a Christian, I appreciate what Muhammad said about himself in the Qur'an – that his purpose was to warn his people that their worship of thousands of deities was in error and that there is only One True God – that being Allah.

4.

Muhammad – one who warned

The Qur'an says:

The Rocky Tract 15:89 And say: "I am indeed he that warns openly and without ambiguity."

The Dominion 67:26 Say: "As to the knowledge of the time, it is with Allah alone: I am sent only to warn ...."

It is also clear from verses in the Qur'an that Muhammad knew of the Jewish and Christian Torah (the 1st five books of the Jewish scripture and of the Christian Old Testament) and of the Injil (the Christian New Testament) and that these writings were to be respected. This is evident in the following sections.

5.

The Purpose of the Taurat (Torah)

The Qur'an says:

The Heifer 2:53 And remember We gave Moses the scripture and the criterion (between right and wrong): there was a chance for you to be guided aright.

The Prophets 21:48 In the past We granted to Moses and Aaron the criterion (for judgment), and a light and a message for those who would do right.

The Bible says:

Joshua 1:8 Do not let this Book of the Law depart from your mouth; meditate on it day and night, so that you may be careful to do everything written in it. Then you will be prosperous and successful.

Psalms 119:130 The unfolding of your words gives light; it gives understanding to the simple.

6.

The Purpose of the Injil (New Testament)

The Qur'an says:

The Family of Imran 3:3,4 …and he sent down the Torah (of Moses) and the Gospel (of Jesus) before this as a guide to mankind ….

The Table Spread 5:46,47 …We sent him the Gospel: therein was guidance and light, and confirmation of the law that came before him.

The Bible says:

Luke 1:3 Therefore, since I myself have carefully investigated everything from the beginning, it seemed good also to me to write an orderly account for you, most excellent Theophilus, so that you may know the certainty of the things you have been taught.

2 Timothy 3:16,17 All Scripture is God-breathed and is useful for teaching, rebuking, correcting and training in righteousness, so that the man of God may be thoroughly equipped for every good work.

7.

The Qur'an confirms Scripture

The Qur'an says:

Jonah 10:94 If you are in doubt as to what we have revealed unto you, then ask those who have been reading the Book from before you....

Winding Sand Tracts 46:12 And before this was the Book of Moses as a guide and a mercy: and this Book confirms it in the Arabic tongue....

With this confirmation in the Qur'an of the Torah and the New Testament as a foundation, Muslims and Christians can also agree, based on their scriptures, that Allah's desire is for us to live good full lives in obedience to the Word of God.

8.

God loves us / God's purpose and plan for us is good

The Qur'an says:

The Heights 7:96 If the people of the towns had but believed and feared Allah, we should have indeed opened out to them (all kinds of) blessings from heaven and earth; but they rejected (the truth), and we brought them to book for their misdeeds.

The Bible says:

Deuteronomy 7:9 Know therefore that the Lord your God is God; he is the faithful God, keeping his covenant of love to a thousand generations of those who love him and keep his commands.

Jeremiah 29:11 For I know the plans I have for you, declares the Lord, plans to prosper you and not to harm you, plans to give you hope and a future.

Galations 5:22-23 But the fruit of the Spirit is love, joy, peace, patience, kindness, goodness, faithfulness, gentleness and self-control. Against such things there is no law.

Revelation 3:19 Those whom I love I rebuke and discipline. So be earnest and repent.

From the foregoing verses, it is clear that disobedience to the commands of God (sin) only serves to separate us from God. Sin corrupts and nothing corrupted can stand before a Holy God.

9.

We are separated from Allah because of sin

The Qur'an says:

The Heifer 2:81 No, those who seek gain in evil, and are girt round by their sins—they are companions of the fire: therein shall they abide (forever).

Muhammad 47:8 But those who reject (Allah)—For them is destruction, and (Allah) will make their deeds go waste.

The Bible says:

Isaiah 59:2 But your iniquities have separated you from your God; your sins have hidden his face from you, so that he will not hear.

1 John 1:10 If we claim we have not sinned, we make him out to be a liar and his word has no place in our lives.

In fact, the Qur'an and the Bible agree that even those we jointly hold in high regard from ancient times fell short of perfection and were guilty of sin. The

following is a list of some of the more notable person-
alities found both in the Qur'an and in the Bible.

10.

Those who sinned

Adam

The Qur'an says:

The Heifer 2:36 Then did Satan make them slip from the (garden), and get them out of the state of felicity in which they had been.

The Heights 7:23 They said: "Our Lord! We have wronged our own souls: if you forgive us not and bestow not upon us your mercy, we shall certainly be lost.

Ta Ha 20:121 ...Thus did Adam disobey his Lord, and allow himself to be seduced.

The Bible says:

Genesis 2:16 And the Lord God commanded the man, "You are free to eat from any tree in the garden: but you must not eat from the tree of the knowledge of good and evil, for when you eat of it you will surely die."

Genesis 3:6 When the woman saw that the fruit of the tree was good for food and pleasing to the eye, and also desirable for gaining wisdom, she took some and ate it. She also gave some to her husband, who was with her, and he ate it.

Noah

The Qur'an says:

Hud 11:47 Noah said: "O my Lord! I do seek refuge with you, lest I ask you for that of which I have no knowledge. And unless you forgive me and have mercy on me, I should indeed be lost!"

Noah 71:26-28 And Noah said: "…O my Lord! Forgive me, my parents, all who enter my house in faith and all believing men and believing women…"

The Bible says:

Genesis 9:20,21 Noah, a man of the soil, proceeded to plant a vineyard. When he drank some of its wine, he became drunk and lay uncovered inside his tent.

Abraham

The Qur'an says:

Abraham 14:35-41 Remember Abraham said "... O our Lord! Cover us with your forgiveness – me, my parents and all believers...."

The Bible says:

Genesis 20:9 Then Abimelech called Abraham in and said, "What have you done to us? How have I wronged you that you have brought such great guilt upon me and my kingdom? You have done things to me that should not be done."

Moses

The Qur'an says:

The Narrations 28:15,16 ...and Moses struck him with his fist and made an end of him. He prayed: "O my Lord! I have indeed wronged my soul! Do you then forgive me!"

The Bible says:

Exodus 2:11-12 One day, after Moses had grown up, he went out to where his own people were and watched them at their hard labor. He saw an Egyptian beating a Hebrew, one of his own people. Glancing this way and that and seeing no one, he killed the Egyptian and hid him in the sand.

David

The Qur'an says:

Sad 38:18-26 ...And David had gathered that we had tested him: he asked forgiveness of his Lord, fell down, bowing, and turned to Allah in repentance....

The Bible says:

2 Samuel 12:9 (Nathan the prophet said to David) Why did you despise the word of the Lord by doing what is evil in his eyes? You struck down Uriah the Hittite with the sword and took his wife to be your own....

Solomon

The Qur'an says:

Sad 38:31-36 ...And We did test Solomon: We placed on his throne a body without life: but he did turn to us in true devotion: He said, "O my Lord!

Forgive me, and grant me a kingdom like which, may not have another ...."

The Bible says:

1 Kings 11:10 Although he (The Lord) had forbidden Solomon to follow other gods, Solomon did not keep the Lord's command.

Therefore, the conclusion to be drawn from the lives of those who have sinned is this: the word "sinner" applies to all of us and none of us can stand before a Holy God on our own merits or credentials.

11.

We have all sinned, all are the children of sinners

The Qur'an says:

The Believer 40:55 Patiently then persevere: For the promise of Allah is true: and ask forgiveness for your fault.

Muhammad 47:19 Know therefore that there is no god but Allah, and ask forgiveness for your fault, and for the men and women who believe: For Allah knows how you move about and how you dwell in your homes.

The Bible says:

Psalms 51:5 Surely I was sinful at birth, sinful from the time my mother conceived me.

Psalms 130:3 If you, O Lord, kept a record of sins, O Lord, who could stand?

1 John 1:8,9 If we claim to be without sin, we deceive ourselves and the truth is not in us. If we confess our sins, he is faithful and just and will forgive us our sins and purify us from all unrighteousness.

These verses from the Qur'an and from the Bible establish that we are all sinners. Our sins separate us from a Holy God. How then can this separation from God, the gap between us and Allah due to sin, be bridged?

12.

Á mediator / intercessor is needed

The Qur'an says:

The Heifer 2:48   Then guard yourselves against a day when one soul shall not avail another, nor shall intercession be accepted for her, nor shall compensation be taken from her, nor shall anyone be helped from outside.

The Cattle 6:70 … But proclaim to them this truth: that every soul delivers itself to ruin by its own acts: it will find for itself no protector or intercessor except Allah ….

The Repentance 9:80   Whether you ask for their forgiveness or not: if you ask seventy times for their forgiveness, Allah will not forgive them….

The Bible says:

Psalms 49:7-8 No man can redeem the life of another or give to God a ransom for him—the ransom for a life is costly, no payment is ever enough….

Matthew 16:26 What good will it be for a man if he gains the whole world, yet forfeits his soul? Or what can a man give in exchange for his soul?

Ephesians 2:8,9 For it is by grace you have been saved, through faith—and this not from yourselves, it is the gift of God—not by works, so that no one can boast.

Hebrews 9:27 Just as man is destined to die once, and after that to face judgment.

From these verses—something to think about: apart from the forgiveness of God—the mercy of Allah—we have no hope.

13.

We need forgiveness to be reconciled to Allah

The Qur'an says:

The Family of Imran 3:135 And those who having done something to be ashamed of, or wronged their own souls, earnestly bring Allah to mind, and ask forgiveness for their sins—and who can forgive sins except Allah?

The Family of Imran 3:193 ...Forgive us our sins, blot out from us our iniquities, and take to Thyself our souls in the company of the righteous.

The Bible says:

Proverbs 14:12 There is a way that seems right to a man, but in the end it leads to death.

Isaiah 64:6 All of us have become like one who is unclean, and all our righteous acts are like filthy rags; we all shrivel up like a leaf, and like the wind our sins sweep us away.

14.

Mercy from Allah is needed

The Qur'an says:

The Women 4:110 If anyone does evil or wrongs his own soul, but afterwards seeks Allah's forgiveness, he will find Allah oft-forgiving, most merciful.

The Cattle 6:12 …He has inscribed for himself (the rule of) mercy. That he will gather you together for the Day of Judgment, there is no doubt whatever. It is they who have lost their own souls, that will not believe.

The Bible says:

Exodus 12:13 (Passover for Jews under Pharaoh of Egypt) The blood will be a sign for you on the houses where you are; and when I see the blood, I will pass over you. No destructive plague will touch you when I strike Egypt.

Matthew 26:28 This is the blood of the covenant, which is poured out for many for the forgiveness of sins.

Titus 3:5 ...he saved us, not because of righteous things we had done, but because of his mercy.

In the next few sections, we will see that Jesus is a central figure in the Christian and Muslim scriptures. It is noteworthy that the Muslims and Christians—based on the writings in their holy books—are in near complete agreement as to the character and unique circumstances of Jesus' birth and life here on earth.

15.

Jesus' virgin birth

The Qur'an says:

The Family of Imran 3:47 She said: "O my Lord! How shall I have a son when no man has touched me?" He said: "Even so: Allah creates what he wills: When he has decreed a plan, he but says to it, 'Be,' and it is!"

Mary 19:20-22 She said: "How shall I have a son, seeing that no man has touched me, and I am not unchaste?" He said: "So (it will be): Your Lord says, 'That is easy for me: and (We wish) to appoint him as a sign unto men and a mercy from us: It is a matter (so) decreed.'" So she conceived him, and she retired with him to a remote place.

The Prophets 21:91 And (remember) her who guarded her chastity: We breathed into her of our Spirit, and We made her and her son a sign for all peoples.

The Bible says:

Matthew 1:22,23 All this took place to fulfill what the Lord had said through the prophet: "The virgin will be with child and will give birth to a son, and they will call him Immanuel" - which means, "God with us."

Luke 1:34,35 "How will this be," Mary asked the angel, "since I am a virgin?" The angel answered, "The Holy Spirit will come upon you, and the power of the Most High will overshadow you...."

Luke 2:6,7 While they were there, the time came for the baby to be born, and she gave birth to her first-born, a son. She wrapped him in clothes and placed him in a manger, because there was no room for them in the inn.

John 1:14 The Word became flesh and made his dwelling among us. We have seen his glory, the glory of the One and Only, who came from the Father, full of grace and truth.

Based on the foregoing verses from the Qur'an and from the Bible, it can be said that Muslims and Christians are in agreement as to the divine intervention surrounding Mary's conception of Jesus. Some claim erroneously that Christians believe that Jesus was born due to a physical union between Allah and Mary. This contention is completely outside the scope of Islamic, Christian or Jewish scripture. The Qur'an and the Bible both state that Mary had not been with a man, yet bore Jesus by the power of the Spirit of Allah.

"Son of God"—This phrase, used in the Christian scriptures in reference to Jesus, is offensive to those who believe it implies that Allah has or had a son in the way that a man has a son. Christians stand with Muslims in rejecting any suggestion that Allah had a son in the physical / mortal sense through a physical union with Mary. Rather, the phrase is used to describe the relationship between Jesus and the Father. How can man understand the nature of Allah? Words are used to convey understanding according to what man is already familiar with in terms of human concepts. For example, how can a man be born from Thunder or how can Encouragement have a child? Note the following verses from the Bible:

Mark 3:17 James son of Zebedee and his brother John (to them he gave the name Boanerges, which means *Sons of Thunder*)....

Luke 1:35 The angel answered, "The Holy Spirit will come upon you, and the power of the Most High will overshadow you. So the holy one to be born will be called the *Son of God*."

Acts 4:36,37 Joseph, a Levite from Cypress, whom the apostles called Barnabas (which means *Son of Encouragement*), sold a field he owned and brought the money and put it at the apostles' feet.

Furthermore, we see that Jesus' name and all the importance associated with it was established before he was born and that he acknowledged it was right to refer to him as the Messiah (the Jewish expected king and deliverer of all men).

16.

Jesus' name

The Qur'an says:

The Family of Imran 3:45,46 …his name will be Christ Jesus,…of those nearest to Allah,…and he shall be of the righteous….

The Women 4:171 …Christ Jesus, the son of Mary, was a messenger of Allah, and his word which he bestowed on Mary, and a Spirit proceeding from him….

The Bible says:

Matthew 1:20,21 But after he (Joseph) had considered this, an angel of the Lord appeared to him in a dream and said, "Joseph son of David, do not be afraid to take Mary home as your wife, because what is conceived in her is from the Holy Spirit. She will give birth to a son, and you are to give him the name Jesus, because he will save his people from their sins."

John 1:41,42 The first thing Andrew did was to find his brother Simon and tell him, "We have found the Messiah" (that is, the Christ)….

John 4:25,26 The woman said, "I know that Messiah" (called Christ) "is coming. When he comes, he will explain everything to us." Then Jesus declared, "I who speak to you am he."

Philippians 2:9-11 Therefore God exalted him to the highest place and gave him the name that is above every name, that at the name of Jesus every knee should bow, in heaven and on earth and under the earth, and every tongue confess that Jesus Christ is Lord, to the glory of God the Father.

From these verses, we see that Muslims and Christians agree that Jesus' name was specifically established by Allah. Moreover, the fact that Jesus did many miracles is recorded in both the Qur'an and Bible.

17.

Jesus' miracles

The Qur'an says:

The Table Spread 5:110 (Allah said to Jesus) "…Behold! I strengthened you with the holy spirit, so that you did speak to the people in childhood and in maturity…and you heal those born blind and the lepers, by my leave. And behold! You bring forth the dead by my leave…."

The Bible says:

Matthew 8:2,3 A man with leprosy came and knelt before him and said, "Lord, if you are willing, you can make me clean." Jesus reached out his hand and touched the man. "I am willing", he said. "Be clean!" Immediately he was cured of his leprosy.

Matthew 8:5-13 When Jesus had entered Capernaum, a centurion came to him, asking for help. "Lord," he said, "my servant lies at home paralyzed and in terrible suffering." Jesus said to him, "I will go and heal him." The centurion replied, "Lord, I do not deserve to have you come under my roof. But just say the word and my servant will be healed. For I myself am a man under authority, with soldiers under me. I tell this one, 'Go,' and he goes; and that one, 'Come,' and he comes. I say to my servant, 'Do this,' and he does it." When Jesus heard this, he was astonished and said to those following him, "I tell you the truth, I have not found anyone in Israel with such great faith. I say to you that many will come from the east and the west, and will take their places at the feast with Abraham, Isaac and Jacob in the kingdom of heaven. But the subjects of the kingdom will be thrown outside, into the darkness, where there will be weeping and gnashing of teeth." Then Jesus said to the centurion, "Go! It will be done just as you believed it would." And his servant was healed at that very hour.

Matthew 8:23-26 Then he got into the boat and his disciples followed him. Without warning, a furious storm came up on the lake, so that the waves swept over the boat. But Jesus was sleeping. The disciples went and woke him, saying, "Lord, save us! We're going to drown!" He replied, "You of little faith, why are you so afraid?" Then he got up and rebuked the winds and the waves, and it was completely calm.

Matthew 9:1-7 Jesus stepped into a boat, crossed over and came to his own town. Some men brought to him a paralytic, lying on a mat. When Jesus saw their faith, he said to the paralytic, "Take heart, son: your sins are forgiven." At this, some of the teachers of the law said to themselves, "This fellow is blaspheming!" Knowing their thoughts, Jesus said, "Why do you entertain evil thoughts in your hearts? Which is easier: to say, 'Your sins are forgiven,' or to say, 'Get up and walk?' But so that you may know that the Son of Man has authority on earth to forgive sins...." Then he said to the paralytic, "Get up, take your mat and go home." And the man got up and went home.

Matthew 11:3,4 When John heard in prison what Christ was doing, he sent his disciples to ask him, "Are you the one who was to come, or should we expect someone else?" Jesus replied, "Go back and report to John what you hear and see: The blind receive sight, the lame walk, those who have leprosy are cured, the deaf hear, the dead are raised, and the good news is preached to the poor...."

We also know from our scriptures that Jesus – unlike any other before him—is described as having the Holy Spirit, is of those nearest to Allah, righteous, holy—without sin.

18.

Jesus' character, life and work — without sin

The Qur'an says:

The Heifer 2:87 ...We gave Jesus the son of Mary clear (signs) and strengthened him with the holy spirit....

The Family of Imran 3:45,46 Behold! The angels said: "O Mary! Allah gives you glad tidings of a word from him: his name will be Christ Jesus, the son of Mary, held in honor in this world and the hereafter and of those nearest to Allah; he shall speak to the people in childhood and in maturity. And he shall be (of the company) of the righteous."

Mary 19:19 He (the angel) said, "No, I am only a messenger from your Lord, (to announce) to you the gift of a holy son."

The Bible says:

Psalms 107:20 He sent forth his word and healed them; he rescued them from the grave.

John 1:1, 14 In the beginning was the Word, and the Word was with God, and the Word was God. - The Word became flesh and made his dwelling among us. We have seen his glory, the glory of the One and Only, who came from the Father, full of grace and truth.

2 Corinthians 5:21 God made him who had no sin to be sin for us, so that in him we might become the righteousness of God.

Hebrews 4:15 For we do not have a high priest who is unable to sympathize with our weaknesses, but we have one who has been tempted in every way, just as we are – yet was without sin.

Again, from their own scriptures, it appears that Muslims and Christians are in agreement that Jesus was holy, righteous—without sin. This fact leads to the question—for what reason did all this take place?

19.

Jesus is the bridge / perfect sacrifice

The Qur'an says: Nothing.

It is at this point that the Muslim and Christian scriptures are clearly not in agreement. The Muslims generally accept that Jesus Christ was a prophet. Christians on the other hand say—yes, a prophet, but also, more than a prophet. Christians believe that Jesus, who was without sin, came for one primary reason. They believe that he came to die on the cross for the sins of all people because man, by his own sinful nature, is not able, nor will he ever be able, to earn his own salvation by doing good works or by any other means. The law, practices and traditions of the Jews since the time of Moses taught them that a sacrifice is needed for the forgiveness of sins. Christians believe that Jesus was the ultimate and final sacrifice for all men for all time and that by trusting Jesus as intercessor / mediator / savior a person is restored to a right relationship with God. Bible verses from which Christians derive this belief follow.

The Bible says:

John 14:6 Jesus answered, " I am the way, and the truth and the life. No one comes to the Father except through me."

Acts 20:28 Keep watch over yourselves and all the flock of which the Holy Spirit has made you over-seers. Be shepherds of the church of God, which he bought with his own blood.

Romans 3:25 God presented him (Jesus) as a sacri-fice of atonement, through faith in his blood....

Romans 5:8 But God demonstrates his own love for us in this: While we were still sinners, Christ died for us.

Galatians 3:13 Christ redeemed us from the curse of the law by becoming a curse for us....

Ephesians 2:8,9 For it is by grace you have been saved, through faith—and this not from yourselves, it is the gift of God—not by works, so that no one can boast.

1 Timothy 2:5,6 For there is one God and one medi-ator between God and men, the man Christ Jesus, who gave himself as a ransom for all men ....

Hebrews 7:25 Therefore he is able to save completely those who come to God through him, because he always lives to intercede for them.

Hebrews 9:22 In fact, the law requires that nearly everything be cleansed with blood, and without the shedding of blood there is no forgiveness.

Hebrews 10:10 ...we have been made holy through the sacrifice of the body of Jesus Christ once for all.

1 Peter 3:18 For Christ died for sins once for all, the righteous for the unrighteous, to bring you to God.

Revelation 19:13 He is dressed in a robe dipped in blood, and his name is the Word of God.

20.

The crucifixion

Certainly here, the two great religions of Islam and Christianity diverge.

The Qur'an says:

The Women 4:157,158 That they said (in boast), "We killed Christ Jesus the son of Mary, the messenger of Allah"—**but they killed him not, nor crucified him** (bold added). But so it was made to appear to them, and those who differ therein are full of doubts, with no (certain) knowledge, but only conjecture to follow, for of a surety they killed him not – no, Allah raised him up unto himself; and Allah is exalted in power, wise.

The following are a few verses from the Bible on which Christians base their belief that Jesus was crucified on a cross, that he died on that cross, and that he was buried in a tomb that same day.

The Bible says:

John 19:16-18 Finally Pilate handed him over to them to be crucified. So the soldiers took charge of Jesus. Carrying his own cross, he went out to the place of the Skull (which in Aramaic is called Golgotha) Here they crucified him, and with him two others—one on each side and Jesus in the middle.

John 19:33,34 But when they came to Jesus and found that he was already dead, they did not break his legs. Instead, one of the soldiers pierced Jesus' side with a spear, bringing a sudden flow of blood and water.

John 19:38-42 Later, Joseph of Arimathea asked Pilate for the body of Jesus. Now Joseph was a disciple of Jesus, but secretly because he feared the Jews. With Pilate's permission, he came and took the body away. He was accompanied by Nicodemas, the man who earlier had visited Jesus at night. Nicodemas brought a mixture of myrrh and aloes, about seventy-five pounds. Taking Jesus' body, the two of them wrapped it, with the spices, in strips of linen. This was in accordance with Jewish burial customs. At the place where Jesus was crucified, there was a garden, and in the garden a new tomb, in which no one had ever been laid. Because it was the Jewish day of Preparation and since the tomb was nearby, they laid Jesus there.

21.

The resurrection

Christians believe that Jesus, after being crucified on a cross and being placed in a tomb, rose from
the dead. Bible verses supporting this belief follow:

The Bible says:

Matthew 28:5-7 The angel said to the women, "Do
not be afraid, for I know that you are looking for
Jesus, who was crucified. He is not here; he has risen,
just as he said. Come and see the place where he lay.
Then go quickly and tell his disciples: 'He has risen
from the dead and is going ahead of you into Galilee.
There you will see him.' Now I have told you."

John 10:17,18 (Jesus said) "The reason my Father
loves me is that I lay down my life – only to take it
up again. No one takes it from me, but I lay it down
of my own accord. I have authority to lay it down
and authority to take it up again. This command I
received from my Father."

John 11:25,26 Jesus said to her, "I am the resurrec-
tion and the life. He who believes in me will live,
even though he dies; and whoever lives and believes
in me will never die. Do you believe this?"

John 20:26-29 A week later his disciples were in the house again, and Thomas was with them. Though the doors were locked, Jesus came and stood among them and said, "Peace be with you!" Then he said to Thomas, "Put your finger here; see my hands. Reach out your hand and put it into my side. Stop doubting and believe." Thomas said to him, "My Lord and my God!" Then Jesus told him, "Because you have seen me, you have believed; blessed are those who have not seen and yet have believed."

Romans 6:9,10 For we know that since Christ was raised from the dead, he cannot die again; death no longer has mastery over him. The death he died, he died to sin once for all; but the life he lives, he lives to God.

1 Corinthians 15:3-6 For what I received I passed on to you as of first importance: that Christ died for our sins according to the Scriptures, that he was buried, that he was raised on the third day according to the Scriptures, and that he appeared to Peter, and then to the Twelve. After that, he appeared to more than five hundred of the brothers at the same time, most of whom are still living, though some have fallen asleep.

1 Corinthians 15:14 And if Christ has not been raised, our preaching is useless and so is your faith.

1 Corinthians 15:17 And if Christ has not been raised, your faith is futile; you are still in your sins.

22.

Those that are Born Again

The phrase, "born again", is commonly used among Christians. It comes from the Christian scriptures and is used to describe a person that believes the Gospel (good news) about Jesus Christ as recorded in the New Testament portion of the Bible. Christians believe a person is "born again" at the point of believing the words of Jesus. Verses from the Bible on which this belief is based follow.

The Bible says:

Matthew 10:32 Whoever acknowledges me before men, I will also acknowledge him before my Father in heaven.

John 3:3 In reply Jesus declared, "I tell you the truth, no one can see the kingdom of God unless he is born again."

John 3:6,7 (Jesus said) "Flesh gives birth to flesh, but the Spirit gives birth to spirit. You should not be surprised at my saying, 'You must be born again.'…"

John 5:24 (Jesus said) "I tell you the truth, whoever hears my word and believes him who sent me has eternal life and will not be condemned: he has crossed over from death to life."

Acts 4:12 Salvation is found in no one else, for there is no other name under heaven given to men by which we must be saved.

Romans 10:9 That if you confess with your mouth, "Jesus is Lord," and believe in your heart that God raised him from the dead, you will be saved.

2 Corinthians 5:17 Therefore, if anyone is in Christ, he is a new creation: the old has gone, the new has come!

Revelation 20:15 If anyone's name was not found in the book of life, he was thrown into the lake of fire.

23.

The Believers

Muslims and Christians however are in complete agreement in their belief that those who trust and obey Allah and seek him with all their heart will be blessed.

The Qur'an says:

The Heifer 2:62 ...and the Christians and the Sabians — any who believe in Allah and the last day, and work righteous, shall have their reward with their Lord; on them shall be no fear, nor shall they grieve.

The Family of Imran 3:114 They believe in Allah and the last day; they enjoin what is right, and forbid what is wrong; and they hasten in good works: they are in the ranks of the righteous.

The Table Spread 5:82 ....and nearest among them in love to the believers will you find those who say, "We are Christians"....

The Gold Adornments 43:81 (Muslims should say to Christians) "If Allah most gracious had a son, I would be the first to worship."

*Consultation 42:*15 …There is no contention between us and you (Jews and Christians). Allah will bring us together….

The Bible says:

Isaiah 41:10 So do not fear, for I am with you: do not be dismayed, for I am your God. I will strengthen you and help you: I will uphold you with my righteous right hand.

Jeremiah 24:7 I will give them a heart to know me, that I am the Lord. They will be my people, and I will be their God, for they will return to me with all their heart.

Jeremiah 29:13 You will seek me and find me when you seek me with all your heart.

Jeremiah 33:3 Call to me and I will answer you and tell you great and unsearchable things you do not know.

Ezekiel 36:26,27 I will give you a new heart and put a new spirit in you; I will remove from you your heart of stone and give you a heart of flesh. And I will put my Spirit in you and move you to follow my decrees and be careful to keep my laws.

Matthew 7:7,8 (Jesus said) Ask and it will be given to you; seek and you will find; knock and the door will be opened to you. For everyone who asks receives; he who seeks finds; and to him who knocks, the door will be opened.

Concluding remarks

Who is a Christian? Though Christian standards in the world are an influence for many good things, some say that pornography, drunkenness, violent crime, abortion and arrogant behavior describe the character of Christian societies today. These things are not supported in Christian scriptures nor do they describe a true believer.

Many who refer to themselves as "Christian" are Christian in name only. They are disobedient to the Word of God and they have not been born again. In all religions of the world, there are those who claim to practice the faith but their hearts are far from the religious teaching and they are not sincere. Christians are not "Christian" because they were born of Christian parents. Each truly believing Christian has sought out the truth on their own and has chosen to believe in Jesus for the complete and eternal forgiveness of their sins. On Judgment Day, Allah will not ask each of us about the family we were born into. No one will be standing there beside us. We will have to give an account for the decisions we have made and the life that we have led.

Muslims—the name given to those who are fully devoted and submitted to Allah—will understand that the term "Christian" has a broad and misunderstood meaning today. According to Jesus, all who place their hope and trust in Him for the forgiveness of sins are saved—no matter what name or title they are using. Muslims and Christians have so much in common. However, they cannot both be right on the question of who Jesus is. Was he truly only a prophet—or indeed more than a prophet—the only One through whom the forgiveness of sins and eternal life can be received? Nevertheless, it should now be clear that Muslims and Christians have many common beliefs. Let us continue to reason together. The greatest blessing and perfect Love of Allah, be yours.

Statements of Faith

The Muslim declaration of faith:
"There is no god but Allah and Muhammad is his Prophet."

The Christian prayer of faith:
"Dear Jesus, I confess that I am a sinner and I believe that you died for my sins on the cross and that you rose from the dead. I now receive you Jesus as my personal Lord and Savior. Please come into my heart, take over my life and fill me with your Holy Spirit. Thank you for setting me free from the guilt and blame for all my sins."